MAKING THE
WORLD
A BETTER
PLACE
WITH YOUR
JOB

By

REV'D ADIEL MARK ISAAC

i

Athor's Contact

Email: rachmieladielmark@gmail.com

Phone: +2348161835845

Published By:

BornLand Media Publishing

BORNLAND WORLD OUTREACH

Email: bornlandltd@gmail.com

TABLE OF CONTENTS

DEDICATION

This book is dedicated to professionals of all works of life across the globe.

ACKNOWLEDGMENT

I sincerely acknowledge and appreciate the Almighty God for the wisdom and grace bestowed on me to put the ideas in this book together.

I further appreciate my lovely parents, late Agent Atemie Mark and Mrs Iseletei. A. Mark, for their overwhelming love and care.

Also, I acknowledge and appreciate my beautiful wife, Nemaloghomabar, for her love and support.

I finally acknowledge and appreciate all those who, in one way or another, had supported me in life and this write-up. May God Almighty bless them all in Jesus' name, Amen.

FORWARD

In a world brimming with challenges, we often wonder how our daily work contributes to something larger than ourselves. "Making the World a Better Place with Your Job" by Rev'd Adiel Mark Isaac is a guiding light, reminding us that every job, no matter how ordinary, has the power to make a positive impact. In the pages of this book, Rev'd Isaac shares practical insights and events that inspire us to rethink the significance of our daily tasks. This book isn't about grand gestures; it's about recognizing the potential for positive change within the reach of our everyday responsibilities.

Rev'd Isaac's straightforward approach invites you to consider the simple yet profound ways your job can be a force for good. It's a call to action, a reminder that you have the ability to influence the world positively through the work you do each day.

May this book inspire you to view your job as more than just a means of earning a living but as a conduit for positive influence. Through small, deliberate actions, you can be part of a ripple effect that contributes to a better world, one that reflects the positive impact each of us can make within the sphere of our daily work.

Wishing you insight and inspiration on your journey to making a meaningful difference through your job.

Peter I. Obioma, (Business and Media Expert).

INTRODUCTION

It is quite obvious that the creator of this universe uniquely designed and made everything beautiful and abundant for enjoyment across the globe.

Judging from the way he designed and made his creatures, in their natures and echelons, the national resources well designed and placed in their unique locations, human resources well created and endowed with his creative abilities and domineering prowess, you can say without mincing words that the creator truly meant well for mankind and the entire world.

The creator of the universe actually multiplied in mankind his creative and leadership abilities to continue the beautiful works of creation, thereby making the world a more unique, peaceful, and beautiful place to dwell.

The creator uniquely created mankind and endowed it with different powerful abilities to think and discover new things and to create, maintain, lead, and organize humans and material things.

The creator made many geniuses and placed them in different fields of endeavor. Some are Engineers, Doctors, Lawyers, Judges, Nurses, Teachers and Lecturers;

Others are leaders, politicians, Business men/women, actors and actresses, manufacturers, and fashion designers; others are security experts, preachers & religious workers, etc.

The creator gave humans all these abilities and jobs to make the world a unique and better place to live.

Surprisingly, the world is gradually becoming inhabitable, a living hell in spite of the huge natural and human resources placed under our control by the creator and the various unique creative abilities reposed on mankind to better the world.

There is the destruction of lives, properties, and even natural resources; wars and insecurity everywhere; hunger, hardship, and poverty almost everywhere; Various sicknesses and diseases bedeviling humans. Bad governments and governance in most parts of the world.

This book is written to re-direct the mindsets of all humans in all works of life, to do the right thing in their daily jobs, and to make the world a better place to live in.

Job is a full or part-time position of paid employment. A piece of work usually at a specific price. It is a specific task people do as part of the routine of their occupation. (MBN 2023).

The regular work that a person does to earn money. (Cambridge Dictionary).

The word "job" was derived from the phrase "jobbe of worke" (1550s), meaning "task, piece of work" (etymonline 2023).

A job is any work or responsibility given to anyone to do in order to have national or financial rewards to make a living.

Jobs can be grouped into three (3) major types:

1. Professional jobs: These have to be done by a well-trained and certified individual. E.g., Doctors, Lawyers, Scientists, Engineers, Lecturers, etc.

2. Trades: These are manual jobs; examples include. Carpenters, auto mechanics, hairstylists, bakers etc.

3. Unskilled, such as farm laborers, cleaners, grocery clerks, maids, etc.

Chapter One

RELIGIOUS WORKERS

As there are many religious bodies across the globe, there are different religious workers employed to keep the organizations going.

A religious worker is a person engaged in and, according to the denomination standard, qualified for a religious occupation or vocation, whether or not in a professional capacity or as a minister (USCIS 2023).

Some major religions of the world include Islam, Christianity, Hinduism, Buddhism, Sikhism, Judaism, Bahai faith, Zoroastrianism, Shintoism, Taoism, Confucianism, etc.

All these religions across the globe have workers who are employed to manage the daily activities of the bodies. They could be employed as ministers, treasurer's secretaries, clerks, bursars, cleaners, yardmen, Sextons, etc.

Every religious adherent believes in the existence of a Supreme Being that they worship and respect and that he or she is accountable to that Supreme Being in whatever they say or do.

Furthermore, this supreme being is a being of supreme justice. In other words, there must be a written order of behaviour from the sacred books of each of the religions of the world that every adherent must follow in order not to incur the wrath of the supreme being that they worship.

All religious workers are flesh and blood living on planet Earth. They are not celestial bodies. So they all owe their creator the responsibility of doing the right things in their duty posts to make the world a better and more peaceful place to dwell.

Religion is the salt of the world that should give good taste to every facet of every society across the globe. Religion is the light of the world that should radiate and remove every darkness and evil around the world. Religion is the peace and morality of the world that should bring peace and decency in all aspects of every society across the globe. Religion is the beauty of every society across the globe. Religion reveals the riches of the creator to mankind and shows the way to enjoy it to the fullest.

But is it like that now? Is religion not bringing cataclysm to the inmates of the world? Is religion not bringing hardships and deaths to humanity? Is religion not bringing laziness to humanity and slowing down progress? Are religious adherents not defrauding and unleashing pain on people?

The world has no taste now and is in turmoil. No peace, No unity, No love, No joy, No justice, No forgiveness, No happiness. Poverty and hardship are everywhere.

Religious leaders and workers are busy doing dirty businesses with religion tarnishing its good Image.

The world is ugly today because religious leaders and workers have failed to do the right thing, and the creator is very angry.

Religious adherents are working everywhere in all industries, both public and private sectors, including all government offices, yet nothing good to show.

WHAT MUST RELIGIOUS LEADERS/ WORKERS DO TO MAKE THE WORLD A BETTER PLACE TO LIVE?

1. A religious worker should note that he or she is a co-creator and maintainer of this universe, not a destroyer.

2. That he is created in the image of the creator to make the world a better place.

3. That he should work by example at the duty post.

4. Religious workers should be very transparent and accountable in management at duty posts.

5. They should be very sincere, regular and punctual.

6. Corruption and partiality should not be seen among religious workers.

7. Religious workers should represent light and good deeds at their designated places of work.

8. Mismanagement and embezzlement of funds should not be heard among them.

9. Religious workers should talk and behave well at their places of work.

10. Religious workers should dress well and be decent at their duty posts.

11. They should be ambassadors of peace and justice.

In all, religious workers ranging from heads to the lowest office holders, should endeavour to show good examples at their working places, and other fields of endeavours will follow likewise, then the world will be very peaceful and a better place to live in.

Religious workers, as a result of their beliefs, are expected to be custodians of moral etiquette that should ignite overwhelmingly high moral standards in all facets of societies across the globe.

Religious workers are called to shine the lights and show the way for others to follow. They are called to make this world a better and more peaceful place to live.

If you are a religious worker, no matter your religion or denomination, you are to make this world a better and more peaceful place to live in with your good deeds, words, and dress.

Know who you are, and gladden the mind of your creator to bless you.

Chapter Two

THE POLITICIANS

Another set of very influential personalities existing in all nooks and crannies of society across the globe are the politicians. They are both in rural and urban settings, and are very powerful.

Politicians are people who are politically active, especially in party politics. Political positions ranges from local governments to state governments, federal governments, and international governments.

All government leaders are considered politicians (Wikipedia, 2023). Politicians have the power to oversee and ensure that public administration is conducted impartially and neutrally.

Politicians organize their daily responsibilities depending on the level of government in which they work. A local politician will likely spend more time face-to-face with community members solving local issues than a national politician who spends time traveling to different states campaigning and meeting with community leaders.

Politicians at any level will generally have a combination of these duties and tasks:

- To interact with constituents.
- To listen to concerns about public issues.
- To serve on committees.
- To write laws

- To create and approve budgets.
- To campaign for votes.
- To give speeches.
- To create jobs for the unemployed youths.
- To provide good social amenities for the public.
- To ensure all institutions in society function adequately.
- To manage all public resources for the good and development of the society.

Political offices include the following:

Councilors, commissioners, Mayors, Governors, Representatives, Senators, Presidents, and Cabinet members.

There are many others who work as politician's staff. They are campaign managers, public relations managers, chief of staff, finance directors, and field organizers.

Politicians are greatly endowed with so many prestigious powers and authorities to transform this world into a paradise. They have all the money and resources at their fingertips. They possess the power to control every other institution in the society. They have the power to compel obedience, discipline erring individuals, and do the right things.

They have the power to instill peace and order in all societies. Furthermore, politicians possess all it takes to employ all the unemployed individuals in society. Politicians have all the resources to provide every good social amenities for the public.

Politicians around the world are the government of the world. They have all the powers to end terrorism and insecurity across the globe.

The issue here is whether these politicians who are wielding so much power are doing the right thing in their various offices. Are they applying political ethos in their adjudication of duties? Why are our societies so much backward, wretched, and inhabitable? Why so much terrorism and insecurity across the globe? Why so much illiteracy, unemployment, and poverty in many parts of the world today? All these and more are questions all political officeholders should ponder and answer.

If only politicians across the globe would understand the prestigious positions the creator has graciously placed them to govern and humble themselves to do the right thing in their jobs, our societies and the entire world would be a better place to live in.

WHAT MUST POLITICIANS DO TO MAKE THE WORLD A BETTER PLACE TO LIVE?

1. Politicians should see themselves as ambassadors of the creator of the world to continue the work of creation.

2. They should note that they will give the account of their stewardship to the creator.

3. They should begin to do the right thing in their positions.

4. They should use the huge resources given for the good and development of the society.

5. They should provide enough social amenities for the general public.

6. They should create employment opportunities and employ the youths, not to make them thugs.

7. They should build good roads, hospitals, and schools and employ capable manpower to Mann them.

8. They should provide adequate security for the general public:

9. They should abstain from corrupt practices and discourage corruption.

10. They should manage our resources well.

11. They should be very transparent and accountable in their administrations.

12. They should love society and the people very well and render adequate services.

13. Politicians should not forget that they have the sole responsibility of turning this world into a paradise with what they do.

You are a politician; you are called not for yourself by yourself but for the general public, society, and the entire world to be happy for you and the creator. So, get to do the right thing now and ever.

Remember, when society is not okay, the poor masses will be hungry and angry, and you and your loved ones will no longer be safe and saved.

You owe yourself and the world the right thing in words and deeds.

Chapter Three

LEGAL PRACTITIONERS

Every society in the world is replete with various gifts, talents, potentials, and brains to make that society and the world a better place to live in when the potentials are properly harnessed and used.

Legal practitioners are very important and influential professionals in every society in the world.

A legal practitioner is an advocate, vakil, or an attorney of any high court and includes a pleader in practice (Lawinsider, 2023).

Legal practitioners interpret laws, rulings, and regulations for natural and juristic persons. Conduct research and gather evidence. Ensure that appropriate approvals are in place before documents are executed. Explaining the law and giving legal advice,others are:

- ✓ To offer legal representation at arbitration or mediation hearings
- ✓ To draft, review, and manage wills, trusts, estates, contracts, and deals.
- ✓ To manage regulatory and compliance-related services.
- ✓ To facilitate innovative solutions to client problems.
- ✓ To offer legal representation to clients in court proceedings on civil or criminal matters.
- ✓ To manage and oversee paralegals and legal assistants.

✓ To Prepare pleadings and notices and make appearances in court. (Betterteam 2023).

In resume, legal practitioners have sacred duties to uphold and observe the rule of law, promote and foster the cause of justice, and maintain a high standard of professional conduct (Djet Lawyer, 2020).

Legal practitioners are inter alia judges, prosecutors, solicitors, ministry officials, court officers, bailiffs, court interpreters, and other professionals involved in the work of the judiciary in the area of criminal law.

The legal profession is a veritable noble profession that possesses the potential to instil justice and foster peace and tranquility that will bring about developments and progress in all societies, making the world a better place to dwell.

There are so many legal luminaries and professionals in all nations across the globe today, yet the world is bereft of justice and peace. Oppression and crime are commonplace. Why? It seems like there is a lacunar of something veritable missing in this noble profession.

It seems obvious that the legal practitioners had deviated from the great ethos of the profession, and the cosmos is in cataclysm.

WHAT MUST LEGAL PRACTITIONERS DO TO MAKE THE WORLD A BETTER PLACE TO LIVE?

Legal practitioners are well placed and endowed as custodians of justice in society to use it to make the world a better place. Legal practitioners should do the following to make the world a better place to live in;

1. They should consider their profession a noble calling from the creator of the universe to bring justice to bare.

2. They should review their professional ethics, removing what is not human/society friendly and upholding what promotes justice and equity.

3. They should absolutely stand for justice and equity no matter what it takes.

4. They should not perverse justice by frivolously basing their judgments on pseudo-verifiable facts but prayerfully investigate to unravel the truth in order to give justice to the oppressed.

5. They should outrightly condemn criminality and crime by giving due punishments to convicted criminals no matter who is involved.

6. Legal practitioners should not be greedy for money and material things so as not to be blindfolded.

7. Legal practitioners must abstain from bribery and corruption.

8. Legal practitioners should do the right thing all the time.

9. Legal practitioners should always be disciplined and be of good behavior, privately and publicly, to maintain a good reputation.

10. Legal practitioners should not be lazy but perform their duties well.

11. Legal practitioners should always dress well to command respect.

12. Legal practitioners should not be drunkards and must abstain from the intake of hard drugs to always have sane minds.

13. Legal practitioners should use their profession to make the world a better place to live in.

14. Legal practitioners should note that, there is a supreme judge, who created and owned this world; he is a supreme being of justice, and a respecter of no one in terms of justice.

In all, the myriads oppressed in the world are looking up to you, legal practitioners, for justice; if you refuse them justice, they might be pushed to take laws into their own hands, thereby making the world unsafe to live in.

This world was created as a paradise, and you must make it with what you do. You have a duty to perform. Doing the right thing is your duty.

Chapter Four

HEALTHCARE PRACTITIONERS

Living healthy and living long in a beautiful world of peace and love is worth aspiring and having.

Healthcare practitioners possess the needed wisdom and knowledge to keep the universe clean and healthy, making it a better place to live in, all things being equal.

Healthcare practitioners are medical professionals who are licensed to provide healthcare services to individuals (Indeed, 2023).

There are multiple types of practitioners, such as medical doctors, osteopathic doctors, nurses, and holistic health practitioners.

They may practice general medicine or focus on a particular specialty. A healthcare practitioner's duties can vary depending on the type of practitioner and their specialization.

Here are a few examples of some tasks a healthcare practitioner may complete:

- ✓ Meeting with patients.
- ✓ Diagnosing health conditions.
- ✓ Performing medical tests.
- ✓ Creating treatment plans.
- ✓ Prescribing medicine or other types of treatment.
- ✓ Coordinating with nurses and other health care professionals to provide quality care for patients.

- ✓ Providing patients with preventive medication.
- ✓ Preventing diseases from spreading.
- ✓ Educating people about prevention, cures, and other such tips.
- ✓ Disseminating information about how to live healthy lives.
- ✓ They help in the delivery during childbirth.
- ✓ They can discover, develop, and manufacture new medication.

Healthcare practitioners determine to a greater degree whether we live healthy and longer on earth or die prematurely.

They are deemed to be the custodians of the world's health. They command so much respect and influence in every society across the globe.

They possess the power to make the world a better place to live. But are they really doing their jobs? Are they doing the right thing at their duty posts? Why are there so many untimely deaths? Why are there so many diseases and sicknesses ravaging the world today? Why are hard and intoxicating drugs commonplace, ruining the lives of our youths across the globe? Why is abortion a destructive menace in many societies across the globe?

It is glaringly clear that something very crucial is missing. Something very pertinent is being left behind by healthcare practitioners. It's like healthcare practitioners are yet to do the right thing as their jobs demand.

WHAT MUST HEALTHCARE PRACTITIONERS DO TO MAKE THE WORLD A BETTER PLACE TO LIVE?

Healthcare practitioners are very pertinent in making this world a better place to live in because they are noble professionals. They should do the following:

1. Healthcare practitioners should know that they are called and gifted in this noble profession to make the world a better place.

2. They should stick to their noble professional good ethos of beneficence, Non maleficence, Autonomy, and justice to make the world a better place to dwell.

3. They should love their jobs and show love to their patients.

4. They should do their jobs diligently and professionally and shun the dereliction of duties.

5. They should note that every individual, whether in the womb or physically, has the divine right to live and should be allowed to live. Discourage abortion.

6. Healthcare practitioners should not love money more than human lives. Save lives first before money.

7. They should spend quality time educating people and the world about health issues to make the world a better place.

8. Healthcare practitioners should abstain from intoxicating substances like hard drugs and alcoholic drinks to have sane minds to attend to patients.

9. They should dress well at duty posts and in other places.

10. They should have good and life-giving temperaments.

11. They should be sincere and hardworking no matter where they work.

12. Healthcare practitioners should know that they are going to give the account of their stewardships to the creator of the universe, who will judge and reward them accordingly.

The world was created and designed for humans to live and enjoy. As a healthcare practitioner, you have a perfect role to play in order to make this world a paradise, and that is, you are doing the right thing in your workplace. Do it, and let's enjoy this beautiful world.

Chapter Five

TRADITIONAL RULERS

The world is made up of different communities to which each individual belongs, and these communities are ruled by natural or traditional rulers who are basically hereditary from those communities where they rule. They are familiar with their subjects, and their subjects know and respect them as well. So, they possess the authority and power to make the world a better place to live in.

Traditional rulers are heads of ethnic units or clans who are, for the time being, the holders of the highest traditional authorities within the ethnic units or clans and whose titles are recognized as the traditional rulers by the government of the state (Law insider 2023).

They are the kings (paramount rulers), chiefs, the executives of the council of chiefs, the community development committees (CDCS), the community women leaders, the youth leaders, and the family executives.

Traditional rulers were regarded mostly as demigods on earth and equally stood in a place of spiritual significance amongst their people.

The roles of traditional rulers include the following:

✓ They chair the meeting of the council of elders of the communities. They do that to formulate and enforce the rules that govern the domain. This really gives direction and political/economic stability in the localities.

✓ They ensure law and order prevail in their jurisdictions. The ideas are communicated mostly via criers, at age grade meetings, and social gatherings summoned by the rulers.

✓ They are the custodians of the cultures and traditions of the land. It is their responsibility to initiate and preside over the celebration of village festivals to keep the culture and traditions of the people intact and sponsor art/culture in their localities to ingrain it in the populace.

✓ They encourage traditional religious beliefs by correcting wrongs and evil doings via the use of gods. The inhabitants of domains abide by the norms and values of the gods.

✓ They oversee chieftaincy matters and confer titles to deserving citizens.

✓ They manage lands and marriage disputes.

✓ They ensure payment of taxes to repair community roads, public schools, and other utilities.

✓ They educate the populace to perform their civic duties.

✓ They get support from their subjects for local council chairmen.

✓ They support good governance by the three tiers of government.

Traditional rulers bring progress and development, which leads to the economic freedom of their subjects (Targba, 2023).

Traditional rulers are natural rulers with powerful influence on their subjects and even government officials because they are their subjects too. They have the influence to attract development to their communities, create jobs for the jobless youths, and maintain order and peace in the various communities.

But why so many communities in darkness? Why so many communities not developed in spite of the huge natural resources inherent? No motorable roads, No good schools for the children, No good healthcare centres, No markets, and No portable drinking water.

Why is there so much restiveness among the youth? Insecurity menace, drug abuse, prostitution, etc.

Why are there so many chieftaincy tussles in our communities? Why is the proliferation of cultism in our various communities robbing the lands of their peace?

It is very obvious that something crucial is missing from the dispositions of our traditional rulers. What could that be? If not that they are not doing the right thing in their domains. And probably doing the opposite.

Traditional rulers such as kings, chiefs, council of chiefs, CDCs, Excos of the youths, and the women's wings should do the 'right thing' in their various domains to make the world a better place to live in.

WHAT MUST TRADITIONAL RULERS DO TO MAKE THE WORLD A BETTER PLACE TO LIVE IN?

Traditional rulers should do the following to make the world a better place to live:

1. They should realize that they are proxies of the creator of the universe in their various domains to make their areas and the entire world a paradise.

2. Traditional rulers should sincerely love their subjects as they love themselves.

3. Traditional rulers should use the resources at their disposal to develop the various communities and their subjects. They should not corner the resources to themselves for any selfish interest.

4. They should not use or manipulate the youths for any selfish interests like gaining and maintaining positions.

5. They should educate the youths and create employment for them.

6. They should influence the government and companies to bring developments to the communities.

7. They should be very sincere in handling chieftaincy issues; truth and justice prevail in all chieftaincy affairs. With this, there will be no need to involve the police or have litigations.

8. They should form a community security and vigilante group to maintain law and order in the communities. They should do everything to discourage cultism, drug abuse, and prostitution in the various communities.

9. They should partner with the government and companies to build good roads, schools, healthcare centres, and other social amenities in their various communities.

10. They should collaborate with good religious organizations to foster peace and development on the land.

11. Traditional rulers should humble themselves, serve the people sincerely, and relate well with them.

12. Traditional rulers should never be selfish but should be selfless as they render their services to the people and their creator.

13. Traditional rulers should note that they are accountable to their creator, who permitted them to be rulers.

Finally, if you rule the people well, they will be very happy, and there will be peace and massive developments. Our communities and the entire world will be a better place to live. Begin to do the right thing now and have a peaceful world.

Chapter Six

EDUCATIONAL PRACTITIONERS

Here is another influential profession that has the capacity to transform the world into a living paradise.

These professionals groom and produce every other professional of different disciplines and enterprises. They are well revered.

Educational practitioners are people who engage in the professional practice of teaching in school settings. They are the teachers and lecturers (Crary et al., 2022).

Below are some of the roles of Educational practitioners:

They inspire, motivate, and encourage a new generation of learners and guide them to make a positive impact in the world.

They help students to be passionate about learning and understand the impact and importance of life-long education.

They act as role models, mentors, caregivers, and advisers, which can have a profound effect on the lives of their students.

They primarily impart knowledge to their students to help them learn new things about a specific group of subjects. "It is the responsibility of the educational practitioners to shape the life chances of young people by

imparting knowledge and bringing the curriculum to life"(Harry Cutty).

They provide social guidance to students.

Educational practitioners play crucial roles in students, parents, societies, and the entire world.

They have the capability to influence and reshape the mindset of future professionals in different fields of endeavours. They also have the power to influence and transform the world into a better and more peaceful place to live in.

When the minds are taught, influenced, and changed, the character and the behaviours will toe the direction of the mindset. If the minds are positive, the dispositions will be positive, too.

This power is given to these educational practitioners to change the world into a paradise. But has the world been a paradise since the inception of this noble profession? Are the mindsets and characters of many people changed positively? Why are there so many illiterates across the globe today? Why are there so many educated illiterates in many parts of the world today? Why are there so many poor and jobless people in most parts of the world today? Why are there so many corrupt minds, including those of this noble profession, in the world today? Why is morality murdered and buried in many parts of the world today?

Something very pertinent is missing here. Examination malpractices are encouraged and promoted in many schools by those of this noble profession in many parts of the world; why?

It is glaringly clear that educational practitioners have left the part of doing the right thing and have taken the ugly part of doing the wrong things. Wrong things like absenteeism from work, dereliction of duty, indiscipline, bribery/corruption, indecent dressing, failure to keep learning and studying, being and showing bad examples to pupils and students, and bad and poor management of schools. Greed, involvement in cult-related activities, involvement in illicit drugs, sex abuse, laziness, etc.

WHAT MUST EDUCATIONAL PRACTITIONERS DO TO MAKE THE WORLD A BETTER PLACE TO LIVE IN?

Educational practitioners should do the following to make the world a beautiful place to dwell:

1. They should be aware that this noble profession is a calling from the creator of the universe to

educate people and make the world a better place to live.

2. They should note that this profession is noble. Therefore, they should love their jobs.

3. They should be hardworking and take their jobs very seriously.

4. They should keep learning and studying to keep themselves updated.

5. They should love the pupils and students and be friendly with them.

6. They should teach very well to cover the scheme of work and discourage examination malpractices.

7. They should teach and promote morality in schools.

8. They should dress decently at work and at home and discourage indecent dressing.

9. They should stay away from cultism as well as discourage it in schools.

10. They should stay away from sexual abuse and discourage it as well.

11. They should have nothing to do with bribery and corruption.

12. They should avoid the intake of intoxicating drinks and hard drugs.

13. They should manage the institutions of learning well.

14. They should not absent themselves from work.

15. Educational practitioners should know that their creator, who gave them this noble responsibility of educating and transforming the world into a

paradise, will require an account of their stewardship from them someday.

If the world is properly educated, evil will decrease, but progress, development, and peace will be the atmosphere, and the world will be a beautiful place to live in.

Chapter Seven

ENGINEERING PRACTITIONERS

Here is another glorified professional with the brains and creative abilities worth transforming the world into an ideal paradise, all things being equal.

With all the natural resources provided by the creator, if properly harnessed and utilized by these practitioners, the world would be a beautiful place to dwell.

Engineering practitioners are professionals who invent, design, analyze, build, and test machines, complex systems, structures, gadgets, and materials to fulfill functional objectives and requirements while considering the limitations imposed by practicality, regulation, safety, and cost (Wikipedia).

They are the automobile, Aerospace, Agricultural, Architectural/Building, Biomedical, Chemical, Civil, Computer, Electrical, Fire protection, Industrial, Mechatronics, Mechanical, Metallurgical/Materials, Mining, and Software Engineers.

These practitioners are working very hard and smart right from inception till date, trying to make things easy-going in this world and influencing the world to appear smarter in all aspects.

They are working so hard and smart, affecting all aspects of life positively and making work easy in working environments with technology. Bravo! to them.

Almost every individual, village, and community across the globe is feeling the impacts of these noble professionals. With their efforts, the world is gradually turning into a paradise technologically. Yet the world is far from paradise in spite of all the effort put in by these engineering practitioners. The world is still groping in darkness and poverty.

The world is still wallowing in immorality. Curable and incurable sicknesses are still killing thousands in the world today. Killings and wars are still ravaging the world. Insecurity and the absence of peace in many parts of the globe. Unhealthy rivalries and competition among many advanced nations.

Why has it been like this all these years in spite of all the good efforts put in place by these smart and industrious practitioners?

Maybe while they put some effort into doing the right thing, the majority of the effort is directed toward doing the wrong things, like:

- Inventing and producing ammunitions and missiles of mass destruction.
- Putting a huge amount of money and resources into inventing and producing destructive weapons instead of inventing and producing life-saving and life-giving materials.
- Failing to uphold engineering ethics.

However, no doubt the facts that some individuals are misusing the good products of this noble profession to make the world a living hell; engineering practitioners need to seriously do the right thing to make the world a paradise.

WHAT MUST ENGINEERING PRACTITIONERS DO TO MAKE THE WORLD A BETTER PLACE?

Engineering practitioners should do the following to make the world a better place to live in:

1. They should realize that they are called and gifted by the creator of the universe to continue the work of creation and make the world a better place to dwell.
2. They should put more effort into inventing, designing, and building infrastructures and systems that support our communities and economies. They should bring new good innovations, developing and improving solutions to the challenges we face now and in the future.
3. They should focus on the invention and production of things that will promote peace and unity and will give life.
4. They should stop the production of materials that destroy lives and properties.
5. They should invent and produce materials that reduce crimes and immoralities in the world.
6. They should stay away from corrupt practices and always maintain integrity in doing their jobs.

7. They should not be greedy for money but with the interest of turning the world into paradise for the benefit of everyone.
8. They should stay away from intoxicating drinks and hard drugs to have the sane minds to do the right thing.
9. Engineering practitioners should bear in mind that they shall all give account of their stewardship to the creator of the universe.

This world is created and given to humans to live and enjoy in peace. Engineering practitioners are given the responsibility of transforming it into a more beautiful place to live in, not a living hell. Begin to do the right thing now to save the world from extinction.

Chapter Eight

ENTREPRENEURS

Financial and material gain is a strong motivational force, propelling individuals, nations, and companies to venture into enterprises to acquire and attain stability.

But should others be hurt, suffer, or die in your bid to acquire them? Money and wealth are good, but should the world be destroyed while you acquire them?

Entrepreneurs are individuals who start or own businesses, whether in farming, retail, manufacturing, or in the service sector. They are business people who find their success by taking risks. In their pursuits, they often become disruptors in established industries (BDC. 2023).

Entrepreneurship is broken into four categories, namely:

Small businesses, scalable startups, large companies or entrepreneurship, and social entrepreneurship.

Entrepreneurs create businesses, create jobs, Develop business plans, employ and manage staff if necessary, Forecast business changes and manage finance, improve the standard of living, and encourage innovation by bringing new ideas, products, and services to the markets.

Entrepreneurs boost the economy of any state or nation. It has the capacity to eliminate poverty by generating employment and stimulating economic activities. Entrepreneurship fosters community development. It increases the gross national product and per capita income of a nation.

Entrepreneurs are vital in societies across the globe. They have the propensity to transform the world into a paradise, all things being equal.

They are functional everywhere across the globe, both in rural and urban areas. They are quite industrious, propelled by the quest to make money and be stable in life.

But the nagging question is, amidst the numerous entrepreneurs in our societies and across the globe, why is poverty still ravaging many parts of the world today? Why is the cost of living so high in different parts of the world? Why is there so much unhealthy competition among some entrepreneurs, companies, and nations that are bringing hardship, deaths, and destruction of properties in many parts of the world today?

It seems there is something very important entrepreneurs are leaving behind. Maybe they are not doing the right thing in their jobs. It also seems they are doing certain things that are not good at all, robbing societies and the world of their beauty. That is why the world is yet to be a better place to live in.

WHAT MUST ENTREPRENEURS DO TO MAKE THE WORLD A BETTER PLACE TO LIVE?

Entrepreneurs should do the following to make the world a beautiful place to live in:

1. They should remember that the creator of the universe called and empowered them to make this world a better place to live by what they do. And that they will be accountable to him.
2. They should work hard to create more jobs for the unemployed youths in society to remove crime in the world.
3. They should think deeply and work smarter to generate economic growth. Identifying opportunities and exploiting them leads to the creation of new businesses and jobs, which will boost national productivity and per capita income.
4. They should be developing new good products and services in all sectors, including health, which will improve the living standard of the world.
5. They should give back to their communities and the world positively by being involved in philanthropy and volunteer work.
6. They should work hard to increase access to education and healthcare, making it affordable for the common man.
7. They should also work hard to make the world more connected.

8. Entrepreneurs should be seriously involved in solving social problems like poverty, hunger, and homelessness.
9. They should improve our environment and the world by protecting energy conservation and pollution reduction.
10. Entrepreneurs should promote peace and understanding among communities, nations, and individuals because, without peace and understanding, their businesses cannot thrive.
11. They should keep empowering women and minorities to start their own businesses.
12. They should consider the well-being of others and the world in their quest to make money.
13. They should subsidize the cost of production and the prices of commodities, making them affordable to the common man.
14. They should stop the production of sub-standard goods that are detrimental to the existence of man.
15. They should avoid unhealthy competition that destroys lives, environments, and properties.
16. They should not be greedy for money by exerting too much profit.

Entrepreneurs should do everything possible to make the world a better place. Do the right thing while making your money. Make others have peace and enjoy this world- You will also enjoy and have peace doing your business.

The world is ours, and we need to turn it into a paradise and enjoy it to the fullest.

Chapter Nine

ACCOUNTANCY PRACTITIONERS

This is another very important set of professionals who have some capabilities to turn this world into a better place to dwell in. Money or finance is well associated with them.

According to the free dictionary, Accountancy practitioners are those who have the requisite skills and experiences in establishing and maintaining accurate financial records for an individual or a business.

Their duties include designing and controlling systems of records, auditing books, and preparing financial statements.

A practitioner may give tax advice and prepare tax returns. They safeguard the integrity of financial reporting. They defend the quality of financial reporting right at the source where the numbers and figures are produced. They contribute to the overall stability and progress of the society.

They adopt a pragmatic and objective approach to solving financial issues professionally. They also offer advice on areas for enhancements. They shape fiscal policies that have far-reaching impacts on the lives of many.

In academia, they are tasked with the important role of imparting the knowledge, skills, and ethical underpinnings of the profession to the next generation.

These practitioners are very involved in everything concerning money, from budgeting to spending and recording. They are in all facets of any society across the globe. Companies, Governments, Businesses, Organizations, and Communities have them.

Money is important to man in life. These practitioners are trained and employed, saddled with the professional responsibility of planning, budgeting, and proper management of funds.

Today, there are so many accountancy practitioners in all sectors of our societies across the globe, yet we hear of poor budgeting and planning, poor or no proper recordings and accountability. Misappropriations, mismanagement, and embezzlement of funds.

People groan and complain about the inhumane behaviors of some of these practitioners in banks and other sectors.

Something very crucial must be missing from these practitioners. And that is doing the right thing. They must have left doing the right thing at their designated working places.

WHAT MUST ACCOUNTANCY DO TO MAKE THE WORLD A BETTER PLACE TO LIVE?

Money is as good as life; accountancy practitioners should do the following right things to make the world a better place to live:

1. They should be aware that this noble profession is a call by the creator to make the world a beautiful and happy place to dwell.
2. They should perform their duties with all sincerity and transparency to have public trust.
3. They should perform their roles with valued integrity, objectivity, and professional behavior to have a better world.
4. They should always display beautiful and welcoming behavior at their places of work.
5. They should not take intoxicating drinks and hard drugs to have the sane minds to do the right thing all the time.
6. They should always dress well.
7. They should always use their words well as they meet with people at their duty posts.
8. They should never be greedy for money.
9. Let them always be open to learning and studying further to help them do their jobs very well and improve the well-being of the world.
10. Let them not only perform duties to improve their lives or their employers, but they should work to improve the standard of living on earth.
11. They should take note that the accounts of their stewardship will be given to their creator by

themselves someday. If they do not perform their duties right, they will cry, but if they perform their duties well, there will be smiling and laughter.

Money is very important to man in life. Good budgeting, management, recording, and reporting will generate joy, peace, and happiness in all sectors across the globe.

But when there is no sincerity, transparency, and accountability, chaos, crisis, hardship, and unhappiness will be the atmosphere across the globe.

The world will be a living hell for everyone. Accountancy practitioners, you are placed well to make the world a better and more peaceful place to live in. Play your roles very well to be well.

Chapter Ten

ARTISTS

This is a beautiful set of professionals in the world that carries a whole lot of weight and influence in every society across the world because, what they do appeals to the very emotional essence of humans.

They have the capability to navigate and determine the mood of humans.

An artist is a person who creates art such as painting, sculpture, music, or writing using conscious skill and creative imagination (Merriam-Webster).

Wikipedia defines an artist as a person engaged in an activity related to creating art, practicing the arts, or demonstrating art.

"Artists' roles are very critical in every society. Creative expression is very vital to a healthy and open-minded society. Artwork inspires people, gives them hope, and can touch a soul in a way that words cannot. The artist has a unique skill set to influence, inspire, and help others" (Christopher J.2021).

"Arts transport people to a favorite memory or a feeling, and it connects people to each other. It starts conversations and relationships." (Richard C.2021).

"Art is a very peaceful, soothing, and comforting form of self-care" (Stacey M.T. 2021).

Furthermore, "Artists bring lightness or introspection to topics that can be heavy and impersonal, to make personal or singular what feels global, immense, and collective" (Lawrence Aczon 2021).

"Artists stand as mediators by nature and human" (Charles Andrade 2021).

More so, artists interpret what is happening in society and the world, helping people digest it"(Megan R. Stern 2021).

Art and artists should have positive effects on our world with the freedom and imperative bestowed on them using their giftedness.

Artists are:

- A vehicle for expressing universal emotions.
- They are responsible for unearthing the truth.
- They illuminate the margins and make societal changes.
- They tell stories and pass on traditions.
- They connect with and inspire people globally.
- They record and preserve our human history.
- They offer messages of hope.
- They are ambassadors of the natural world.
- They create a sense of community.

The different types of artists are painting, illustration, sculpture, visual 3D, graphics and animation, literature, architecture, film, music, Theatre, and fashion.

All these are gifted by the greatest Artist and creator of the universe to make the world a unique and better place to live in.

But where are we now? Are artists really making the world beautiful or ugly? Are the works of art actually promoting morality or immorality in the world? Are the artists and their acts promoting peace or crisis in all societies across the globe?

Why is the surge of immorality and indecency in the world today? Social media today is replete with disgusting phonographic works of art.

Indecent dressing pervades the air. Many artists are veritable tools of propaganda in the hands of some avaricious fellows, inciting unrest in many parts of the world. Many music artists and entertainers have replaced morality with immorality by what they sing and act.

The world is no longer sane and safe to dwell in. Something very important is not being done by our amiable artists. Doing the right thing is the thing.

WHAT MUST ARTISTS DO TO MAKE THE WORLD A BETTER PLACE TO LIVE IN?

1. Artists should know that they are co-creators with the creator of this universe, and their responsibility is to make this world a better place to live in.
2. They should begin to do the right thing in their work to affect people's lives and the world positively.

3. They should avoid being used to create propaganda, no matter the financial rewards.
4. They should avoid painting or creating phonographic images arousing immorality.
5. They should avoid writing, singing, and performing songs that promote immoral behavior.
6. They should dress decently and promote decency in all ramifications.
7. They should abstain from the intake of hard drugs and intoxicating drinks to have the right minds to do the right things.
8. They should respect their creator and the giver of their gifts to excel.
9. They should be more creative to make the world a beautiful place to live in.
10. They should be good role models to affect the younger generation positively, to have a better world to dwell in.
11. You are an artist, and your unique duty is to make the world a beautiful place to live in. Keep to your good duty and role, no matter the enticing pay to deviate. This is our world; we need to make it better than we met.

Remember, you must give the account of your stewardship to your creator sometime, someday. Behave well and be better.

Chapter Eleven

FASHION DESIGNERS

Here is another set of hardworking personalities with the capability of transforming this world into a beautiful place to live in.

Wikipedia defined fashion designers as those who create clothing for consumers, including dresses, suits, pants, skirts, and other accessories like shoes and handbags.

Furthermore, fashion designers sketch designs of clothing, footwear, and accessories. Fashion designers create original clothing, accessories, and footwear. They sketch designs, select fabrics and patterns, and give instructions on how to make the products they design (Career 2023).

A fashion designer is a creative professional who develops original concepts for clothing, shoes, and accessories. They may specialize in clothing for men, women, or children or build brands in other categories like evening wear, sports Wear, swimwear, maternity, intimate apparel, or sleepwear. After conducting research and sketching drafts on paper or computer applications, they then sew or manufacture their designs from various fabrics and materials. They may also create designs for mass production and sale in boutiques or other retail stores (Indeed, 2023).

The typical duties of fashion designers can vary based on the particular markets they serve. For instance, a fashion designer who specializes in designing luxury high-fashion formal wear for celebrities may have different duties than a designer who creates everyday looks for retail customers. Here are some typical fashion designer duties:

- They conduct research into fashion trends and consumer behaviors to find inspiration.
- They create and label preliminary sketches of fashion pieces with colour and material ideas.
- They find, develop, and choose the appropriate fabrics, patterns, and materials for designs.
- They visit textile providers, manufacturers, and trade shows to source unique supplies.
- They cut and sew fabric and other elements into an initial prototype of the design.
- They conduct model fittings to adjust designs for production or for display in fashion shows.
- They supervise pattern makers, sewers, and tailors in manufacturing prototypes and final items.
- They oversee the mass production of their designs to ensure adherence to the vision.
- They develop new designs and fashion lines for new seasons, holidays, and social periods.
- They attend fashion shows and other industry events to market designs and brands.

In summary, fashion designers make clothes and wears to cover human bodies from the crown of the head to the soul of the feet, giving the body beautiful fittings and protecting the body from cold and heat. The creator of the universe and the first perfect fashion designer first designed and made clothing from leaves and covered the nakedness of Adam and Eve as recorded in the holy Bible.

He also dressed his Angels with beautiful apparels. The creator of the universe knew the need to cover human bodies and make the bodies more beautiful to behold; that was why he replicated himself in fashion designers, to continue the good works of making beautiful clothing and wears for mankind. He really hates it when humans parade themselves naked and dress indecently.

Today, what do we see in the name of fashion? What do fashion designers produce today that is really or gradually transforming the world backward to the Adamic age? In the name of fashion and modernization, gullible and vulnerable humans are rooming the streets naked, like we are in a crazy world, promoting indecency and immorality. Our eyes are seeing what our mouths cannot say anymore.

Delicate parts of the human body are now exposed, attracting so many rape cases. The world is no more safe and beautiful to live in.

WHAT MUST FASHION DESIGNERS DO TO MAKE THE WORLD A BETTER PLACE TO LIVE IN?

1. Fashion designers should know that they are ambassadors of the creator and the first fashion designer; they should represent him well by doing the right thing.

2. They should design and produce clothes and wear that will cover the human body properly. One can appear very sexy in beautiful clothes that cover the whole body. They should stop promoting indecent dressing by what they make. They should stop promoting immorality by what they design and produce.

3. They should use their job to make the world a better and more beautiful place to live in by designing and producing the right clothes and wear for both sexes.

4. They should always dress well to show good examples.

5. They should know that all shall give account of their stewardship to the creator of the universe.

Covering our bodies with good and beautiful clothes and wear makes us feel good and healthy. The world will be very peaceful and beautiful to live in.

Let fashion designers begin to do the right thing and make the world a better and more beautiful place to live in.

Chapter Twelve

SECURITY AGENCY

We are living in a world where some humans are so problematic and cannibalistic by whatever that makes them.

Most strong humans would not let the weak be. Many are so greedy and rapacious that they would rob, steal, maim, kidnap, and even kill others for whatever gains they aspire to.

Many others are filled with the spirits of vandalism, whereby valuable properties are being destroyed daily in many parts of the globe.

Security of lives and properties is a very pertinent part of society across the globe.

According to Wikipedia, a security agency is a governmental organization that conducts intelligence activities for the internal security of a nation. They are the domestic cousins of foreign intelligence agencies and typically conduct counter-intelligence to thwart other countries ' foreign intelligence efforts. For example, the United States Federal Bureau of Investigation (FBI) is an internal intelligence, security, and law enforcement agency, while the Central Intelligence Agency (CIA) is an external intelligence service that deals primarily with intelligence collection overseas. A similar relationship exists in Britain between M15 and M16.

Every nation across the globe has security agencies to maintain law, peace, and order. Some have more than ten. For example, Nigeria has (10) security agencies, namely:

1. Department of State Services (DSS) in charge of protecting state institutions and properties. Investigating and preventing crimes against the state. Protecting the president, vice president, and other senior government officials. Providing security for foreign dignitaries visiting the country. Maintaining internal security.

2. The Nigeria police force (NPF), which is responsible for law enforcement and maintaining public safety across the country. They are also in charge of criminal investigations. They have a large number of officers, with over 350,000 currently on staff.

3. National intelligence agency (NIA) with the sole responsibility of gathering and analyzing intelligence related to national security. It has an approximate staff of 5,000 people and is divided into four directorates: The directorate of operations, Intelligence, administration, and research.

4. Economic and Financial Crimes Commission (EFCC), which looks into financial crimes like money laundering, advance fee fraud (419), and embezzlement. It has the power to freeze bank accounts, confiscate assets, and prosecute offenders.

5. Independent Corrupt Practices and Other Related Offences Commission (ICPC) is an anti-corruption agency established to investigate and prosecute all corrupt practices and offences in the public and private sectors. Its main objective is to promote transparency and accountability in the management of public resources.

6. Code of Conduct Bureau. An agency that is responsible for enforcing the code of conduct for public officers. It makes sure that everyone is following the code. It is also responsible for investigating allegations of misconduct against public officers. It also makes sure that all public officers declare their assets and income to ensure that they are not accumulating wealth unlawfully.

7. The Nigeria security and civil defense corps (NSCDC). This is a paramilitary organization that is set up to protect the country against internal and external threats. They are responsible for border security, counterterrorism, and emergency response. It has over 170,000 members.

8. The Nigerian Army is responsible for land-based operations.

9. The Nigeria Air Force is responsible for the protection of Nigerian airspace and the conduct of air operations in support of internal security. It has more than 10,000 personnel.

10. The Nigeria Navy has approximately 15,000 personnel and 110 vessels protecting the nation's maritime interests.

What baffles me most is that, in spite of all these security agencies across the globe, there is a myriad of security threats arising from emerging technologies, climate change, terrorism, and economic fault lines (Indian View, 2023).

Human lives and properties are no longer safe in this world. Robbery, kidnapping, vandalism, terrorism, killings, wars, Money laundering, and cultism still threaten our existence today. We have so many security agencies everywhere, yet we live in terror. What are all these security agencies actually doing?   No peace almost everywhere.

I think these security agencies are not doing the right thing. They have gone far, neglecting to do the right thing.

Many parts of the world are a living hell. It seems no place is safe anymore. The lands and roads, our seas and creeks, the air and space, our towns and villages are well occupied by men of the underworld.

WHAT MUST SECURITY AGENCIES DO TO MAKE THE WORLD A BETTER PLACE TO LIVE IN?

1. Security agencies should know that they are called by the creator of the universe to protect lives and properties and to maintain peace and order across the globe in order to make the world a better place to live.

2. They should resist negative influences from groups and individuals that will make them deviate from their primary assignment of making the world a better place to live in.

3. They should refuse to collect bribes from any individual or group that will make them shirk away from their responsibilities.

4. They should give their minds to studies to acquire the required knowledge to address the evolving security challenges bedeviling mankind proactively.

5. They should not love money and material gains.

6. They should fear no one except the creator of the universe.

7. They should abstain from taking intoxicating drinks and hard drugs to enable them to have the right mind to do the right things.

8. They should live by example and never compromise their responsibilities.

9. They should not promote insecurity by patronizing criminals and cultists.

10. Those recruited to serve should be of noble character and reputation, not questionable behavior.

The world would be a better place to live if all security agencies across the globe respect lives and properties, and diligently do their jobs with all sincerity.

The creator of the universe is also the owner of lives and the universe. We need to protect and secure human lives and the universe, behaving well and doing the right thing, no matter what.

Knowing fully well that everyone will give an account to the creator someday, including all security agents. Behave well and do the right thing now.

Chapter Thirteen

CRIMINALS

There are many other things some people do that are against humanity and society. Either they do as a source of income, a means of livelihood, or for pleasure and fun, and for ritual purposes, making the world a living hell.

Collins English dictionary online defines a criminal as a person who regularly commits crimes.

There are many and various crimes against humanity across the globe. See the list below:

1. Cybercrime is doing something illegal over the internet or a computer. Hacking and defrauding people, causing pain to unsuspecting fellows. Many have died, and others are groaning in pain for these criminal acts.

2. Organized crime is the transnational, national, or local grouping of highly centralized enterprises run by criminals for the purpose of engaging in illegal activity, most commonly for monetary profit. Many are victims of this kind of crime and are in agony.

3. Violence and crime, which focuses on homicide and sexual assaults, which have really robbed humanity of life, Joy, and peace.

4. Robbery: FBI defined robbery as the taking or attempting to take anything of value from the care, custody, or control of a person or people by force or threat of force or violence and or by putting the victim in fear. This criminal act has really caused and is still unleashing mayhem on humanity and societies across the globe.

5. Drug trafficking: This is the illegal importation, manufacturing, transportation, distribution, and possession of unlawful controlled substances such as cocaine and heroin.

6. Arson is the malicious, intentional burning of a building or other structures.

7. Money laundering is a crime involving the movement of illicit money and other gains into legitimate channels in order to disguise the money's illegal source and thwart tax officials.

Kidnapping, Terrorism, Murder, Theft, and child abuse are some of the crimes perpetrated on Earth against humanity, making living on Earth unbearable.

Crime is a major part of every society. Its costs and effects touch just about everyone to some degree. The types of costs and effects are widely varied. In addition, some costs are short-term, while others last a lifetime. Of course, the ultimate cost is loss of life. Other costs to victims can include medical costs, property losses, and loss of income. Loses to both victims and non-victims can also come in the form of increased security expenses, including stronger locks, extra lighting, parking in more expensive secure lots, security alarms for homes and cars, and maintaining guard dogs.

Considerable money is spent to avoid being victimized. Other types of expenses can include a victim or person fearful of crime moving to a new neighborhood, funeral expenses, legal fees, and loss of school days.

Some costs of crime are less tangible (not easily or precisely identified). These kinds of costs can include pain and suffering and a lower quality of life. There are also the traumatic impacts on friends and the disruption of family. Behavior can be forever changed and shaped by crime, whether it be weighing the risks of going to certain places or even the fear of making new friends.

Crime not only affects economic productivity when victims miss work but also affects communities by the loss of tourism and retail sales (encyclopedia.com).

In this world, everyone must have to do something to make a living or survive for the short period we live on earth. There are many legitimate and good jobs to do for a living rather than indulge in criminal activities that affect the perpetrators, victims, and the entire universe.

If one is affected and angered by the injustice done to him, resorting to criminal activities as a payback should never be an option or solution. There are other legitimate ways to express your emotions rather than being involved in crime destroying oneself and society at large.

Things are very hard and difficult in the world today, yes, but does that justify killing humans for ritual purposes, kidnapping for payment, cheating, stealing, robbing, and assassinating people for survival?

If you are offended and angered, that does not give you the right to kill, destroy, and terrorize society. We are all humans, for God's sake, created in his image. We are meant to work hard and be our brother's keeper.

This world is given to us to live in peace and enjoy it. Remove greed and the mentality of getting rich quickly from you.

Patiently work hard and smart in your legitimate endeavors. Be proactive and sincere in getting what you want without inflicting pain on your fellow humans.

As you legally work very hard and smart in all your endeavors, depend on your creator and the creator of the universe for success.

Let us all work hard to make this world a better place to live in. Criminality will never do you or anyone good.

CONCLUSION

Our maker and the creator of this beautiful universe never made any mistake in creating and making us inmates of this world. He made it for us to live in harmony and peace and enjoy to the fullest.

No matter our geographical locations, complexion, languages, cultures, religion, and differences, we are one beautiful product of the creator who made us to enjoy this beautiful world.

Making this world a beautiful and better place to live in is no one person's job. It is our job and collective responsibility to make it better.

Use your God-given gifts and talents rightly and correctly to beautify and make this world a better place to live in.

It is super correct to make money and earn a living with what you do, but while making your money, do not harm and hurt others. Do the right thing always, no matter your profession.

Whether in private or public sectors, domestic workers and housewives, politicians and government functionaries, and traditional and religious leaders/workers, let everyone begin to do the right thing to make the world better than we met.

Let all criminals, scammers, fraudsters, rapists, kidnappers, ritualists, terrorists, etc., turn a new leaf and begin to do the right thing to make this world a better place to live in.

Governments and world powers should do everything to make peace and stop wars/ conflicts bedeviling most parts of the world.

We are one people with one creator who gave us this beautiful world. Let us all have Love and live in Unity, not minding our diversity.

Doing the right thing always is the only way to make the world a better and more beautiful place to live in. Let's do it now. This is our world, our home, our place, and our joy.

WORKS CITED

D.Harper, *"Job"*, Etymology, 2023, etymology.com

"What is job," Market Business News, Sept. 2023, marketbusinessnews.com

"Major religions of the world" Info please, Sept. 9, 2022, infoplease.com

"Chapter 2 -Religious workers" Policy Manual, Sept. 2023, USCIS.gov

"Politicians," Wikipedia, accessed 3 Oct. 2023, en.m.wikipedia.org

"Roles and responsibilities of politicians and Bureaucrats," Japan kantel, 16 Sept. 2009, japan.kantel.go.jp

"Roles and responsibilities on a politician's staff," Indeed, Accessed 3 Oct.2023, www.indeed.com

"Political Ethics," Wikipedia, accessed 3 Oct. 2023, en m wikipedia.org

"Legal practitioner-Definition," Lawinsider, accessed 4 Oct 2023, www.lawinsider.com/dictionary

"Lawyer job description," Betterteam, Accessed 4 Oct 2023, www.Betterteam.com

"An Appraisal of the Duties of Practitioners under," djetlawyer, 23 April 2020.

William P. Alford et al, *"Legal Ethics,"* Britannica, 29 August,2023.

"How to Become a healthcare practitioner in 10 Steps," Indeed, 3 March 2023, www.indeed.com

"Who is considered a healthcare provider/ practitioner?" UC Berkeley, Accessed 5 Oct 2023, hr.berkeley.edu

"What is the role of Healthcare professionals?" St. Patrick's, Accessed 5 Oct.2023, www st.patricks.ac.uk

"Pharmaceutical scientist," Explore Health Carears, Accessed 6 Oct 2023, explorehealthcarears.org

Ethics in Healthcare, "Improving patient outcomes," Tulane University, Accessed 7 Oct 2023, publichealthtulane.edu

"Targba B," *The roles of Traditional rulers in Nigeria ",* First Class Nigeria, Accessed 7 Oct 2023, Firstclassnigeria.com

Sarah L Clary et al, *"What is Education practitioner?"* igi-global, 2022, www.igi-global.com

"What are the roles of an educator in school?" Total Jobs, Accessed 9 Oct 2023, www.totaljobs.com

"Code of Ethics," National Society of Engineers, accessed 10 Oct 2023, www.nspe.org

"What is an entrepreneur?" Business Development Bank of Canada, Accessed 12 Oct 2023, www.bdc.ca

"4 types of entrepreneurship; which one is right for you, Boise State, Jan. 2019, Boise state.pressbooks.pub

Raz Yosef; *"What are the significant roles of an entrepreneur?"* Onpassive, 22 August 2022, www LinkedIn.com

"10 important roles of an entrepreneur," Indeed, Accessed 12 Oct 2023, www.indeed.com

"Top 9 effects of entrepreneurship on economic development," Emeritus online courses, Accessed 12 Oct 2023, Emeritus.org

"How do entrepreneurs make a difference?" Calendar App, 13 June 2023, www.calendar.com

"Accountancy practitioner," The free dictionary, Accessed 20 Oct 2023, legal-dictionary-*thefreedictionary.co*

"What does an accountant do? Role, and responsibilities" University of the Potomac, accessed 21 Oct 2023, potomac.edu

"Artist definition and meaning," Marriam-Webster, Accessed 21 Oct 2023, www.merriam-webster.com

"Artist", Wikipedia, accessed 22 Oct 2023, en.m.wikipedia.org

"What is an artist's role in society?" Frame destination, accessed 23 Oct 2023, www.framedestination.com

"Katie C." What is the artist role in society?" Artwork archive, 24 Oct 2021, www.artworkachive.com

"What kind of artist would you be?" Superprof, Accessed 23 Oct 2023, www.superprof.com

"Fashion design," Wikipedia, Accessed 24 Oct 2023, en.m.wikipedia.org

"Fashion designers", Occupational Outlook handbook, Accessed 24 Oct 2023, www.bls.gov

"Should I be a fashion designer? 10 reasons to pursue this role," Indeed carear Guide, 1 Oct 2022, www.indeed.com

"Security agency (organization type)," Wikipedia, accessed 26 Oct. 2023, en.m.wikipedia.org

"The top 10 security agencies in Nigeria," Within Nigeria, Accessed 26 Oct 2023, www.withinnigeria.com

"Global security challenges in 2023," The Indian View, Accessed 26 Oct 2023, natstrat.org

"Criminal" Collins Dictionary, Accessed 27 Oct 2023, dictionary.com

"Patrick Murray," *What are the 20 most common types of crime in the UK?"* Criminal Law, 2 Nov 2021, Britton time.com

"Economic and social effects of crime," Encyclopedia, Accessed 27 Oct 2023, www.encylopedia.com